Rented

Poems on prostitution and dependency

Rented – Poems on prostitution and dependency

First edition 2018 from Palewell Press www.palewellpress.co.uk
Reprinted 2023 by Palewell Press

ISBN 978-1-911587-08-8

The cover design is Copyright © 2023 Camilla Reeve
The photos on the front and back cover are Copyright © 2023 Eugene
Homewood

A CIP catalogue record for this title is available from the British
Library.

Palewell Press

Rented

Poems on prostitution and dependency

Sue Johns

Prostitution is not just a service industry, mopping up the overflow of male demand, which always exceeds female supply. Prostitution testifies to the amoral power struggle of sex, which religion has never been able to stop. Prostitutes, pornographers, and their patrons are marauders in the forest of archaic night.

Camille Paglia

Dedication

Dedicated to Patric, Agnes and Katy for their poetic support
and to the wonderful Eugene for life support.

Acknowledgments

'The Goose the Ghost and the Man' appeared in *Trespass* magazine, 2012.
'Watching Promise' was published as a members' prize poem in *Poetry News* 2017.
'Before the Pussy Riots', 'Remembering Mrs Lot' and 'Instructions for a Summer Wedding' all appeared in *Loose Muse* anthologies by *Morgan's Eye Press* 2012-2014. 'God Said' appeared in *Prole* magazine 2017.
'The Goose the Ghost and the Man' and 'The Dancer's Choice' were also published, by artist Lorraine Clarke, as part of an exhibition in 2014.

Contents

The Goose the Ghost and the Man

The Clink was my manor where I still reside with the whores
(The Winchester Geese), the paupers, the dispossessed.
In the still of a 21st century Sunday to the rattling of trains,
in the shadow of The Shard, through the countless
skulls and syphilitic bones, it is as goose I rise.

Not a bird fattened in the cloisters destined
for a Christmas plate, I am heroin chic,
super model thin as I slip through *The Red Gates*.
I caress its ribbons, poems, its tiny bears, a shrine
to the 'working girls' homespun and trafficked.

From my sisters of the past to those
who trade on the pavements of London,
Birmingham, Nottingham. Snuffed out
like the candles nestling in the weeds they
will burn again as the stones are turned to beating organs.

I honk and glide over the rooftops, the narrow
streets no longer running with stinking waste,
over the Bishop's ruins whose coffers
held the rent from the lodgings
where I spread my legs.

Over the market where I sold myself
at Southwark Fair. The wharfs that knew
mob rule, that rocked to music
and pleasures of the flesh, now
sterile boxes to seal the wealthy off.

Hissing over the singing Thames
to the seats of government, law, and finance -
the old haunts of the father I never knew.
I seek a certain type of gentleman.
I enter the safe sleep of lawyer, judge, stockbroker, priest.

In dreams they wrestle me in my room
at *The Anchor*, their portly bodies
enfolded in my wings. With a scratching in their groins
they awake perspiring on feather pillows
beside their cold and tidy wives,

dress to face an innocent morning, soap
me from their shiny skins. In hangman tight
ties, mildly harassed by the half-digested grass
upon their stairs they pause in doorways,
prepare to stride their importance into the light.

Before I launch, take flight to *Crossbones*,
their feet embed themselves in my excrement,
with a final twist of my elegant white neck
I rip through expensive shoe leather
and peck at their adulterous heels.

*Crossbones Cemetery is the sight of a medieval burial ground in
Southwark, London. Originally created for prostitutes known as The
Winchester Geese, after The Bishop of Winchester whose title permitted
prostitution on the South bank, for 400 years, in return for rent from
the brothels.*

Floralia

Is this the day of my honorable death?
The beasts are slain and now
the arena heralds man to slaughter man.
Must melancholy stain this tainted liberty?
Slave sisters, this is your time.

Leave your stone-cold beds in the fornices,
flesh and fluidity are the weapons you deploy.
The wind has swept the blossoms from the hillside,
the violets lie crushed by frozen rain.

Revive each rose upon the cheeks of an emperor,
bare your breasts for Flora and the mob,
let coloured cloth unwrap your nakedness. Go!
Sex the buds that will rupture sod –
the gods are the exponents of your wantonness.

Stir wombs under a shower of garbanzo,
rebirth, as I allow *The Circus* to do its worst.
Dance! Fornicate!
And may the frenzy you create ensure the bay
stays evergreen, to deck each favoured crown.

Floralia was an ancient, Roman festival held in honour of the goddess
Flora. Prostitutes led most of the celebrations.

Stag

The groom gets a rough crossing
in a shirt bearing **Stevies Stag** –
no apostrophe. A swaying
of medieval alleyways awash with neon.

With the last Heineken barely
punching the gut and the briefest glimpse
of the wares in a reddened window
he gets man-handled through a door
for an *early wedding present.*

Teodora *Not your real name.*
Yes my real name, after the saint.
Her body is blasphemy, her beauty
breaks the dawn over De Wallen
as the first trams ring out from Damrak
resounding like a Sunday morning.

As wedding heels are worn-in
hard, pink shellac taps out the final list.
Over prosecco a brood of hens
lay their plans of lace and cake.

for the over-fed lamb who will be
already bound as he waits at the altar.
His shoes, as grubby as ternate futures
and a trousseau of euros in a bedroom drawer.

Rented

That kiss was not the debutante's kiss
bought at De Beers
then deposited in the 'country pile.'

That kiss was certainly not the girl's kiss
purchased with ponies and funds in trust.

That kiss was not the kiss
in the back of the Daimler
that never was a kiss
but something more urgent
exchanged for a single note.

That kiss, one of many kisses
you will deliver in this stuccoed hallway,
was the 'boyfriend experience.'
Your manly hands enfolding his face,
your tongue at the back of his throat.
Such a kiss my dear, can only be rented.

A Friend of Promise

She was interrupting the stacking of Tampax,
waiting to receive her little cup of Meth
with one hand holding 'trackies' around
her skinny, white hips.
Ola and I exchanged raised brows.
I remember that, but not exactly when it was
that I decided to steal her. Or why
her in particular. Was it because she lived
across The Square? Or because she was
much younger than us other 'working ladies'?

But not too young to go 'doctor shopping', though.
She'd just traded one addiction
for another. I prayed over her
and on the third day of her sweaty sentence
she took a little jollof rice and soup
but I knew, when she ate my chicken stew,
the girl was clean.

'Clean enough to visit home' she said
'Come with me to The Chilterns,
fields and hills' she said.

She didn't need to explain why we didn't make it.
I heard it all on speaker-phone,
you won't bring drugs into this house,
or those people either,
so we are to stay with her aunt in Southampton.
I asked if we'd still get fields and hills.
She said 'Promise, we will' and even better
she said 'We'll have the sea,
we'll have real fish and chips
and we'll have sailors.'

Watching Promise...

across The Square,
from under the tabby nets,
it seems a client has left her a gift.
My guess is a filthy finger nail
got married to her oily hip
and fathered some pus just out of reach
because she's using some dirty dance-moves
to squeeze it.

Promise knows this isn't like the hand-jobs
we give, off the kerb, ending in a heavy spurt.
This is a wound that'll spread
and come back weeping across an angry border.
It reminds me of those new girls,
when they stray into a foreign postcode.

Promise needs to put on the slippers
that make her look free again
(though she's formidable in heels)
and pay a visit to the prissy chemist

who will be relieved (not,) to be asked
for 'Morning Afters' or a cream for 'crabs',
though she'll still dispense that look
she reserves for an entire continent
watching Promise, bounce her box-braids
out of there with a crash
and the door-bell pinging.

This is our healing-time.
My friend rubs antiseptic
into the wet of her back-fat as The Square
takes a communal draw to the lungs,
watching Promise unlock her milky windows
to lie with her legs wide open
and let in some air.

Words that Promise Knows

WANTON:
A brazen *ashewo*,
who did not go home
to 'lay out' her mother.

WON'T:
The oath,
the pledge of disallowing,
the things she *no go do.*

FAITH:
Her allegiance to Jesus,
her belief *that betta don come.*

FACE:
No dorti slap,
her pan cake,
her beautiful gap-tooth smile.

PASSPORT:
Corner, corner,
a visa,
a key,
her safe conduct.

PASS OUT:
When she get *shayo*
and bury her pain.

CAN'T:
All of the impossible,
the bodi no bi firewood.

CUNT:
Or *kpekus.*
No matter the word -
they *go do am* again and again.

WANT:
She want *God go butter her bread*
and no more men
erect as headstones.

Before the Pussy Riots

1.

The brightly balaclava'd
ventured, where intrigue capered
amongst the bells and incense.
Unorthodox then
for punks
to dance and pray
to Virgin saints.
When can their glory fade?
Oh what a charge they made
Those girls, sentenced to sew
the warp of unease
only discarding
the weft of corruption
to queue for gulag fare
in lines as crisp
as Stalinist snow.

2.

To be violated was as criminal
as it was to love for
the believing women,
who draw their outer clothes
around them,
that they would be recognised
and not molested.
Freedom was claimed
in dreams, behind bars
and beneath burkhas
as their learned sisters
took to the skies
with the speed of flying acid -
their pages bullet-ridden,
their faces a curse upon
the naming of schools.

3.

It was written that
the nature of women
was to seduce men.
But the sound was red
as a naked girl hit the dust.
When her honour soaked the ground,
in a continent of coloured silk,
there was none to cover her.
The Preserver and
The Conqueror of Ignorance
were as any other idols -
bedecked with flowers,
being offered a light lunch
while Eve was teased.
Justice was measured in media coverage
as a dowry purse was counted
and a husband reached
for kerosene and matches.

Alfred, Lord Tennyson (The Charge of the Light Brigade)

The Quran 24.31

Manusmriti 2.213

14

God said...

that I am stranger than the honey on my lips.
My mouth is as smooth as oil -
easing me, along, to a bitter end.
These stilettos are bound for hell.

I say 'Couldn't your son wash his own feet?'
'Don't bring my hair into it
I'm dry-eyed and my perfume stays
right behind my ears.'

My attic brings salvation to many men
and my walls don't even crack.
This town isn't Jericho, baby -
I can worship the moon if I wish.

There is no faith to save me
I will not go in peace.

Remembering Mrs Lot

But his wife looked from behind him, and she became a pillar of salt.
Genesis 19:26
Come, let us make our father drink wine, and we will lie with him, that we may preserve the seed of our father. **Genesis 19:32**

You always looked over your shoulder –
checking my movements.
On our ungodly streets you turned
to the sounds of sodomy and sucking

so we silently closed our doors
and conceived our daughters, shrouded,
in the dark. They grew with a passion
alien to their begetting and strode before us

from our city in flames. It was then
that I whispered "Do you not wish
to see how all that irks you burns?"
You could not resist, and I laughed

at your pale pillar- the art of our maker
without mercy. I laugh as our offspring
ply me with wine - I have been drinking
their beauty for years.

And I take them, our angels,
held by the hair they will not turn
just writhe and work themselves a lineage
as I lick their bodies free of salt.

The Rock Hits the Spot

The rock hits the spot and makes me feel. Dizzee
Rascal sings *Scream and Shout*- from the radio -
in this car. I'm warm but business aint easy.

My man sends me out with a slap. Those filthy
punters are plenty, that's three in a row.
The rock hits the spot and makes me feel dizzy.

I need to 'scrub up' my skin feels so itchy -
sores on my cheeks, pus dries on the pillow
my forehead is warm, this business aint easy.

I've tried to leave - get away from - that greasy
Pimp - blacked my eye and fractured my elbow.
The rock hits the spot and makes me feel. Dizzy

drunks, over Christmas, are all kissy, kissy -
revellers drinking to turkeys and snow -
leave me beer, it's warm and business aint easy.

Mates hand me tights freshly nicked out of Sainsburys,
we cut the crotches for access below.
The rocks hit the spot and make us feel dizzy.
Our legs may be warm but business aint easy.

Instructions for a Summer Wedding

When your ancient spouse lies beneath the earth,
the scholars will permit a *Misyar* husband to take,
and leave you, as he pleases. Reconcile the frailties

of the first love he leaves at home. To your children
he is neither blood nor provider. Have them hushed
and hidden until you charm your permanence into his

rationed heart. Keep safe the wedding papers for when
they come to accuse you as a whore. Observe the flocks
of widows, as they peck amongst the garbage,

in the slums of Riyadh. And if winter finds you
cold and empty in your bed, behind the Souk
the women may sell their possessions.

Educated and beautiful? You are desirable as
a *Misyaf* wife. Name your price for European travel -
to protect your makeshift husband from the temptations

of the West. Steer misguided hands to your rented hips
and forbidden hair. Make the comforts of a lover as accessible
as room service. Check your reflection in a Knightsbridge

window. Know that Chanel smells of jasmine and roses
but that gold and loneliness have no aroma. Conceal your tears
in designer purses. Shroud before landing. Pack-up

your killer heels. Back-seat drive your gifted wheels
to Jeddah market. Check the melons have over ripened -
confirming that Summer is over.

Misyar and Misyaf are temporary marriages popular in Saudi Arabia

The Doctorate

For Belle de Jour

Sweating the men from my pores,
I could afford the heating again,
had a 'good bottle' on ice.
I remember being so sore from a spanking,
courtesy of Mister G, I'd had to stand to read
'Statistic Method in Genetic Epidemiology'.

Discovering that, post Chernobyl,
most thyroid cancers in Cumbria
occur in women under twenty four
as I remember the Wednesdays
that I'd helped Edward, from his sticks, onto the bed -
he could never complete the act.

Julian's food fetish, what a memory -
cream, live yoghurt, baked beans (never own brand).
All had sounded a death knell for my silk camies.
I was his sweetheart not fished
from the sea of digits in Mister G's black book.
He got, all night, to remind me who was paying.

Walking clean and sensibly-shoed
into the world of child health,
still wearing red underwear,
I remember going into 'the black'.
Kicking off my stockings and stripper-heels
as STD checks were exchanged for charting PCB's.

Holding back cancers I learn that
Edward is 'no longer with us' from the girl
who induced his final, contented moans.
Always the gentleman he'd waited to die at home.
I remember his sexual preferences
as I data based gene patterns and clinical trials.

These days only my books are leather-bound.
At the back of the closet are a few clingy
'numbers' teased in like memories.
As I cut off a final old tie
I hear Mister G got fucked by the recession -
now, if he's lucky, he can rent by the hour.

The Dancer's Choice

She was *pliés* and poses, applause
and Tchaikovsky. *Pas de chat*
Sleeping Beauty. Chocolates and bouquets
outside the Opera House.
Always *on pointe* for gentlemen callers.

Post war chic - Piccadilly, Mayfair.
But one small slip and something's
missing. Counting the weeks,
squeezed in a costume. *Pas de cheval*
Sleeping Beauty.

She knows someone who knows
someone. Not telling anyone
getting it fixed. But inside Aurora
another ballerina
is already cast as the Lilac Fairy.

Her steps are perfect *piqué, piqué*
Aurora doubles over. Away from the *barre*
arabesque and retch. With the dilation
they'll expose the little dancer,
cauterizing her pirouette.

Down in the basement
is the shell-shocked assistant.
A perfectly recruited victim of the trenches.
He'll never speak of the baby *protégée.*

Writhing in the gore, gauzed
in lavender. Right on cue,
rising from the sluices,
leaving the sink with a *grande jeté.*

Looking for Calamity

Calamity was not brought up with protection from the evils of the world...she was not immoral but unmoral, with her upbringing how could she be anything but...she was a product of the wild and wooly west – **Dora Du Fran (1868-1934)**

We were both whores at fourteen but your face
was taking on a cow's arse by the time we met.
So I became a Madam and you became a man.

They're still making shows out of you, girl,
much prettier tales than your own.
Some, kind of, mimic your cussing and drinking

but, mainly, you've become a whip-cracking blonde
with hands on hips and eyes shining
and I never knew you could sing.

You worked in a crib at Three Mile Hog Ranch -
twenty soldiers in a night, still in their boots
Tougher 'n' hell and to hell with the consequence.

You figured *If a girl wants to be a legend*
she should just go ahead and be one.
But the bottle took all six foot of you down.

So where is the real Martha Jane
gone, with the shit, from the streets of Deadwood,
gone with the dead eyes of laudanum?

Where is my illiterate black-eyed girl,
my prairie dove with a love of whiskey
who just did, what poor girls did, back then?

The Emperor's Bed

My pillows are bitten by the chosen -
the lotus footed conveyed by eunuchs.
Vermillion ink has recorded
their cherry-lipped, pale-faced presence
in a city where you are never alone.

Those new-moon virgins were gone
before my dragon-eyes opened -
the silk already bloodless.
Long before the sun echoed from the mirrors
the golden curtains had released their prisoners
all arched brows and dripping jade.

With my sovereign at prayer
my coverlets lie pristine and waiting.
My regal frame accepts the incense from the courtyard,
a gift from an ancient Cypress.
My mahogany is mute and shining –
built to take and give nothing away.

Star - for Billie Holiday

I know crying won't change a thing
I sang my way to hell
And back again
I'm always making a comeback
But nobody ever tells me where I've been.

Gave my young body for dollars
It seems my soul was
Never worth a dime
Don't threaten me with love, baby
Let's just go walking in the rain.

I went from jail to Carnegie
But couldn't sing away
The ball and chain
I'm always making a comeback
But nobody ever tells me where I've been.

Men and the needle unease me
The night brings back the dawn
With all its pain
Don't threaten me with love, baby
Let's just go walking in the rain.

Lines above in italics are quotes from Billie Holiday

Domestic

Having decided to make love
in our galley kitchen, we realise
not every dish has to start
with garlic and onions.

The stove is out of bounds -
harbouring our nourishment
contained in something heavy,
foreign, built to outlast us.

Do you see, through the porch window,
the bulbs that have survived the frost?
As you issue over the recycling.
Watch me ape

along the Edwardian door handles
until you find the place
like the natural break in asparagus.
You wipe clean the Perspex bar-stool

as I rest in the adjoining room.
It had offered us soft furnishing,
a comfortable landing. We are spent
and have saved the upholstery.

Cur

There has been a number of instances of criminal damage to trees in this park...caused by dog owners training certain breeds to attack trees...trees are now dying as a result of this. **Extract from a sign in a London Park**

Do you miss the birdsong from the Crabapple?
Remember the confetti from the Hawthorn
and Cherry, proclaiming Spring,
before the Mastiffs stripped them bare?

I have packed away the picnic rug,
the wicker basket and the paper cups
since the Hounds took to hunting the Ash and the Elm
under which we shared sandwiches and wine.

I knew when the Lap-dogs came
out from under the skirts of dowagers,
jumping and swinging from the burnished branches,
there would be no more Chestnuts on the fire.

And by the time you read this the Bull Terriers
will have warred with the Holly and Mistletoe.
There will be no greening of mantels this Christmas -
our kisses will flounder under distressed pine.

Hamster Time

They relied on us for seed, and shavings of wood.
We could turn their day to night
at the drop of a blanket -
start them where we left off, on the treadmill,
marking time, going nowhere,
busying on our behalf.

They didn't live long; biennially we removed
a cold corpse from the straw.
Our tower block home
prevented burial; everyone was tearful
unaccepting of the deaths
the dustbin was out of the question.

We magnetized them.
Placed upon our fridge:
Fluffy reminded us to buy butter and eggs,
Honey sat stiff on the bills in red,
Tiny timed the school runs,
Cheeks's rigor mortis held dentist appointments.

But dead hamsters don't last forever,
their fur fell out along with their eyes,
decomposing paws dropped
our lives onto the lino.
Minus these reminders
we lost our sense of purpose.

The lights went first and then the heat,
we took our children out of school,
stopped shopping for food,
scavenged in cupboards
opening tins with our teeth
which eventually, without due care, we lost.

Communicating in squeaks,
pausing to defecate in corners,
we formed our wheel from bedsteads and bikes
then with uncut nails we set upon the piles
of junk-mail and papers
and constructed the ultimate nest.

Hormonal Sentience

Bush walk, South Africa

Trees are telling tales –
murmuring to the neighbors
in ethylene, to fill their leaves with tannin,
make themselves distasteful
to hungry browsers.

Trees speak, as they did
when man's mimicry
was all but animal.
In the days of stone shapes
and fire miracles. When language
rolled in with the wheel.

Mopane trees; added their tongue
to the clicking consonants
of Khosian, the long Dutch vowels.
When the first ship anchored
at The Cape and unloaded its cargo
of dubious futures.

Acacia trees; wept with
The Abolitionists, mused
on the passing of mules and wagons,
the death of each warrior,
every red-coated column
and debated the true price of gold.

Trees, in yellow-flowered frocks,
gossiped and prayed each summer
long, sang anthems, cast
their ballots in the breeze.
As freedom was islanded
in the time of monochrome.

Trees, with rebel pheromones,
collude at sunrise.
When shots ring from the mines
and each thrumming shanty
surrenders its contents
to the needs of the sparkling towns.

Hormonal Sentience: Information exchange between plants

Catching Up

My dear, how I miss you.
Your mother has shown me a photo,
you are so thin, we worry that you are not eating.
You say it is because of all the running along the Hudson -
you run so much you do not have time to walk
to the East Village for pierogi instead
someone drives sushi to your home.

I will never be thin my love,
though here, in Ukraine, I am always running:
running to my second job,
running from the police across the Maidan,
running from the wild dogs
that live behind our apartment.

Now I am standing in the kitchen, breathless,
but tonight I may go dancing.
I hear you have a new woman, who is also thin.
Are you dancing with her my darling?
Are you dancing with that empty skirt?
I have one hand on my hip, the curves you once admired,
with my other hand I am stirring borscht
so thick I can draw a round face on its surface.
I do not think it is yours.

Speed Walking with Baby

I watch the world whoosh! Snug in my merino wool.
Pastel shades compliment a streamlined chassis
locked into its off-road wheels.

Hold on Dada! As you hurtle me,
your muscles rejoicing in the underfoot comfort
of a two-layer, mid-sole construction.

Propelled by her pelvis, Mama keeps up
burning the carbs but with the trickery
of a sweat wick, she merely glows.

In the triple-glazed nursery mobiles hang,
struggling, save for my post-traumatic breath.
There's a lesson in my dreaming -

trees can fly with the birds and skyline,
children and dogs communicate
in snatched one-liners,

everything outside is fast and furious -
to the beat of a father's footsteps
and the meter of a mother's swinging hair.

The Road

Footballs, bicycle wheels,
footballs, the family business,
footballs, my heart snagged on the gorse,
footballs.
All lost on The Road.

If you hand-held your life
you could cross The Road
into your grandparents' garden,
catching your breath on fried bacon,
through the cowpats and caravans
and over the *One Mile of Golden Sand*
as far as France.

Or be sand-scooped into a VW
by a teenage surfer
and delivered home for a lecture
over a tea of wet ham.

Away from The Road,
in the eternal sunshine,
farm dogs dizzied around babies
in 'Silver Cross' prams.
The stream, waged in tadpoles,
serenaded the schoolyard,
post office, church.

Drowned out on The Road,
a chorus of neighbours.
It's a death trap, that road
It had made a career of murder:

Seagulls, foxes,
badgers, rabbits,
impatient motorists, my brother,
caterpillars, assorted pets.

I took The Road
returned when speed-restrictions
and time had done their taming.
Offered my hand to The Road -
it takes so little now.

Sue Johns – Biography

Sue Johns lives in London but originates from Cornwall where she started writing and performing as a 'punk poet.'
She also writes and performs theatrical monologues and works with art/word collaborations.

Publications by the author include a collection *Tantrum* 1998 and a pamphlet *A Certain Age* 2003. Her collection *Hush* was published by Morgan's Eye Press in 2011.

Information at http://www.suejohns.co.uk

Palewell Press

Palewell Press is an independent publisher handling poetry, fiction and non-fiction with a focus on human rights, social history and the environment. The Editor can be reached via
enquiries@palewellpress.co.uk